TIME FOR KIDS READERS

MW00358589

Native Americans

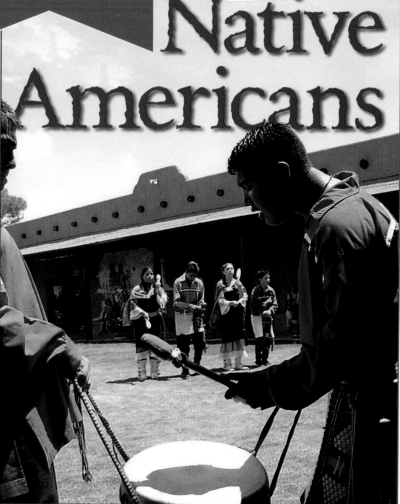

by Angela Shelf Medearis

Harcourt

Orlando   Austin   Chicago   New York   Toronto   London   San Diego

Visit *The Learning Site!*
www.harcourtschool.com

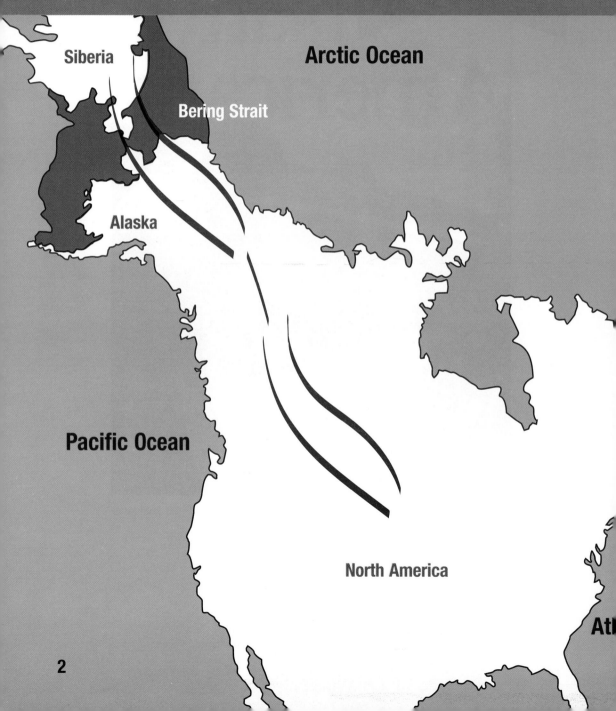

The land bridge under the Bering Strait and the seas around it are thousands of miles wide. The black lines on the map below show the path taken by people and animals who crossed the land bridge into North America thousands of years ago.

Siberia

Arctic Ocean

Bering Strait

Alaska

Pacific Ocean

North America

At

The Long Journey South

From Siberia in the vast northeast region of what is now Russia to Texas—that's a long, long way to travel. That is, however, the route some scientists believe the ancestors of Native Americans took 40,000 years ago.

Thousands of years ago, thick layers of ice covered great areas of land in northern Asia and North America. So much ocean water was frozen that the sea level dropped. Today, the waters of the Bering Strait separate Siberia and Alaska. Back then, the sea level was so low that Siberia and Alaska were connected by land. The path between them is called the Bering Land Bridge. The first Native Americans traveled across this land bridge into North America.

Those early natives moved from place to place in search of food. They walked across the land bridge to hunt giant elephant-like animals called mammoths and mastodons. As the number of people grew, the natives separated into hundreds of different groups. Moving farther south and east, these separate groups of people eventually reached nearly every corner of North, Central, and South America. Each group developed a way of life unique to the area in which it lived.

Woolly mammoths grew up to 12 feet (4 m) high and weighed more than 15,000 pounds (6,800 kg).

cean

The First Texans

The first Native Americans arrived in Texas about 13,000 B.C. By the 1500s, when Europeans first came to Texas, Native Americans there were organized into hundreds of different groups—bands and tribes. Each had developed its own society, culture, and religious practice. Each group had learned how to adapt to the various regions in Texas where they settled.

The largest groups of Native Americans lived in several different parts of Texas. The Comanches (kuh•MAN•cheez) lived on the Southern Plains. The Apaches (uh•PA•cheez) settled mostly in the mountainous and desertlike areas of the Big Bend. The Tonkawas (TAHN•kuh•wuhz) occupied much of the central Texas Hill Country. The Karankawas (kuh•RANG•kuh•wawz) lived along the Texas coast. The Coahuiltecans (koh•uh•WEEL•tuh•kuhnz) lived in the Lower Rio Grande area of South Texas. The Caddos (KA•dohz) lived in the Piney Woods region. At one time, about 45,000 Native Americans lived in Texas. By the middle of the 1800s, only a few thousand Native Americans remained.

What happened to all these Native Americans? The first European settlers in Texas were from Spain. At first, they thought it was best to keep peace with Native American tribes. After all, there were only a handful of Europeans in Texas and many Native Americans. Instead of fighting the Native Americans, the Spanish tried to get them to give up their traditional ways of life. They wanted the Native Americans to work for them on their farms and as house servants. Priests were brought in to get them to accept a new religion. Many tribe members died from diseases brought by the Europeans.

In the early 1800s, settlers from the East were pushing the Native Americans from their tribal land in Texas. The Native Americans often fought in wars against settlers and United States soldiers.

By the last part of the 1800s, most Native Americans in the United States had been forced to live on reservations—land owned by the United States government and reserved for them. Many tribes were moved to reservations in Oklahoma, New Mexico, and Texas. Most of the major Native American groups that lived in Texas before the European settlers arrived were gone.

IT'S A FACT

In the Caddo language *tayshas* meant "friend." Spanish explorers thought *tayshas* meant "land," and over time, *tayshas* became pronounced *Texas*.

The Disappearing Tribes

Throughout the United States, diseases and wars with soldiers and settlers killed hundreds of thousands of Native Americans. By 1900, only 250,000 Native Americans remained in the United States. Since then, the number of Native Americans has increased. The 2000 census counted almost 2 million Native Americans in the United States. Texas now ranks fourth in Native American population with about 118,000 Native Americans living there.

The tribes that live on reservations in Texas are the Alabama–Coushattas, the Tiguas, and the Kickapoos. The Black Seminoles is another tribe with members who live in Texas.

This Comanche chief and his people fought settlers who wanted to claim tribal land in Texas.

A member of the Alabama-Coushatta tribe wears traditional clothing at a festival in Texas.

The Alabama-Coushatta

The Alabamas and the Coushattas are two different Native American groups. However, they have lived closely for a long time and have a similar language, so they are considered a single tribe. Originally, both tribes were members of the Creek tribe that lived in the southeastern part of the United States. This area would become the states of Alabama, Mississippi, and Georgia.

In 1541 the Spanish explorer Hernando de Soto became one of the first Europeans to make contact with the Alabama tribe in what is now Mississippi. Over the next 100 years, the Alabama tribe moved into the territory that would one day be named after them. At about this time, members of the Coushatta tribe set up villages near the Alabama tribe.

Eventually, white settlers began moving into areas where the Alabama and Coushatta tribes lived. In 1763 the tribes decided to move westward across the Mississippi River to Louisiana. In the 1780s the tribe moved again, this time across the Sabine River into Texas, which was ruled by the Spanish. Many of the tribe settled in a region called the Big Thicket—a heavily forested area of southeastern Texas. That is where most members of the Alabama-Coushatta tribe live today.

The Alabama-Coushatta reservation was formed in Polk County in 1854. The United States government granted the tribe 1,111 acres of land near the town of Livingston, Texas. About 3,000 more acres were added in 1928. That land has provided the tribe an income through the sale of lumber. Although they cut down trees, the tribe still respects the land and works to conserve it. Proof of that came when their timber program won Texas's top award for forestry conservation.

Income also comes to the tribe from tourism. Money from those sources and the U.S. government has been used to help support the tribe's schools and community projects.

The Tiguas

The Tiguas are part of the Pueblo tribe. Today, most of the Pueblos live in New Mexico and Arizona, but their lands once stretched through Colorado, Utah, and West Texas. The Tiguas live on a reservation in El Paso—the only members of the Pueblo tribe still living in Texas. Though surrounded by other cultures, the Tiguas have managed to preserve their way of life.

The cultural center on the Tiguas' reservation includes a museum. Visitors can see women prepare food in adobe ovens similar to ones used by their ancestors. Celebrations include traditional dances that have become popular El Paso events. Tiguas have built their houses in the style of the Pueblos. Some of the original Pueblo houses were more than 40 feet (12 m) high and looked like apartment buildings.

Like their ancestors, many Tiguas are farmers. They grow corn, beans, and squash. Some of the older Tiguas wear clothing made of leather and animal furs, as did their ancestors.

This is a meeting house on the Tiguas' reservation in El Paso, Texas.

The Tiguas are famous for their pottery, which they used for cooking and storing their food.

Until the 1930s, few people in Texas knew that the Tiguas even existed. Over the years the tribe had lost much of its land. In the 1960s the Tiguas began to reclaim some of the land that belonged to their ancestors. Finally, in 1968, the Texas government granted the Tiguas full recognition as an official Texas Native American tribe. President Lyndon B. Johnson signed a bill in Congress that made the land the Tiguas lived on a reservation. Tourism has been a source of jobs and income for the Tiguas for many years. The tribe has created businesses as well, such as a factory that dries chilies for sale. They also work with several large agricultural companies.

Handpainted pottery by the Tiguas is known for its beautiful designs.

The Kickapoos

Today, there are fewer than 1,000 members of the Kickapoo tribe. They live in parts of Texas, Kansas, Oklahoma, and northern Mexico. At one time, the Kickapoos were part of a larger Algonquian-speaking tribe that lived in the Great Lakes region of the United States.

In the 1800s the Kickapoos left the Midwest and divided into three groups—the Kansas Kickapoos, the Oklahoma Kickapoos, and the Mexican Kickapoos who are also known as the Texas Band of the Oklahoma Kickapoos. The Spanish government asked the Mexican Kickapoos to settle in Texas. The Spanish hoped the tribe would help them prevent settlers from the United States from entering Texas, but the settlers continued to arrive. Later, the Kickapoos were forced out of Texas and settled across the border in northern Mexico. Eventually, they came to live in the Mexican city of El Nacimiento.

The Kickapoos' home is Mexico, but they don't stay there all year. During the spring, many Kickapoos travel through Texas and other western states working on farms. By the end of October, they begin returning to their homes in Mexico to farm and hunt.

In 1983 the United States officially recognized the Texas Band of the Oklahoma Kickapoos as a Native American tribe. The 800 members of the tribe raised money to purchase 125 acres near Eagle Pass, Texas, in 1984.

The Kickapoos have a special status. They are treated as if they are citizens of both the United States and Mexico. The Kickapoos do not consider themselves citizens of either country. They think of themselves only as Kickapoos. They can cross the U.S.-Mexican border without any restrictions, and they are allowed to find work in both countries. Kickapoos do not have to license their vehicles in Mexico, and they can buy items without paying import taxes.

Of all of the Native American groups in North America, the Kickapoos have been among the most successful at retaining their old traditions. Throughout their history, Kickapoos have refused to mix any outside culture with their own culture. The Kickapoos—especially those in Mexico—live the same way that they have lived for hundreds of years. They usually marry only within the tribe. Their children do not receive education by the government. Instead, they are taught by tribal elders. Although the outside world has had some effects on them, the Kickapoos continue to remain true to their traditions.

A photo taken in about 1900 shows Kickapoo children playing outside their homes in El Nacimiento, Mexico.

This Kickapoo Indian grew up on the Kickapoo reservation near Eagle Pass, Texas. The building behind her was once her family's home.

The Black Seminoles

In the late 1600s a number of enslaved Africans from the English colonies began escaping to Florida, which was under the control of Spain. At the same time, Seminole Indians also began settling in Florida. Seminoles were members of the Lower Creek Native American tribe. The Seminoles bought some black slaves and also received slaves as gifts from the British, who took over Florida from Spain in 1763.

Being a slave to the Seminoles was very different from being a slave in the British colonies. Seminole slaves weren't harshly treated, and sometimes they even became members of the tribe. The Seminoles gave the enslaved Africans tools to build houses and to raise their own crops. When the crops were harvested, the Seminoles accepted a reasonable part of the crop for payment. The enslaved Africans kept the rest. The Seminoles allowed them to have their own livestock from which they only took a small part. This relationship helped the Africans as well as the Seminoles. The Africans needed protection from the white plantation owners who wanted to take back former slaves by force.

Africans and Seminoles lived separately from each other and had their own chiefs, but they became friends. Some Seminoles and Africans married and started families. Their children were called Black Seminoles.

Problems came when the United States went to war to take possession of Florida from Britain. At the end of several long, brutal wars with United States troops in the 1800s, Seminoles and Black Seminoles were forced to leave Florida for Arkansas and Missouri.

A Black Seminole chief named John Horse led his people to Oklahoma and then across Texas to Mexico. Eventually, the U.S. Army hired Black Seminoles to be Indian scouts and soldiers in West Texas. Their unit was called the Black Seminole Scouts. The scouts' knowledge of English and Spanish and their experience in warfare made them great fighters against other Indian tribes in the 1870s. After several battles, four members of the Black Seminoles won Congressional Medals of Honor.

Rose Fay, a Black Seminole, was photographed at her Texas home in 1937.

12

TFK
IT'S A FACT

Over thousands of years, many Native Americans have lived in Texas. Some were in large groups called tribes, which were ruled by chiefs and had a common culture. Smaller groups were often called bands. These are some of the Native American groups, large and small, that have lived in Texas.

Alabama-Coushattas	Choctaw Chickasaws	Lipan Apaches
Apaches	Coahuiltecans	Shawnees
Atakapas	Comanches	Tiguas
Black Seminoles	Delawares	Tonkawas
Caddos	Karankawas	Wichitas
Cherokees	Kickapoos	

Bud Crockett holds a photo from the 1800s of his great-great grandmother, Dora Davis. Crockett's ancestors were Black Seminoles, some of whom came from Texas. Today, Crockett lives in Wewoka, Oklahoma.

During the 1870s, the U.S. government wasn't sure if the Black Seminoles should be considered African Americans or Native Americans, who had the right to live in the Indian Territories. Some Black Seminoles became tired of waiting for the government to make up its mind. They left Texas to live in Mexico. Other Black Seminoles went to live in communities of freed black slaves. The rest of the Black Seminoles stayed at Fort Clark in southwestern Texas until the Black Seminole Scouts were disbanded in 1912.

About 200 to 300 Black Seminoles moved to the nearby area of Brackettville. Today, a small community made up of the descendants of the Black Seminoles live in this south Texas town. Sometimes, Black Seminoles from Texas meet with Black Seminoles who live in Mexico and Oklahoma to celebrate their common culture.

These Black Seminole army scouts were photographed at Fort Clark in about 1885. Descendants of some of these men still live in southwestern Texas.

15

In Del Rio, Texas, a grandmother teaches her granddaughter the traditions of the Lipan Apaches.

Although these are some of the most recognized tribes of Native Americans living in Texas, descendants of many other Native American tribes live there. The people in most of these tribes, however, are widely scattered throughout the state. Many have been completely absorbed into modern society.

As time goes on, though, more people are beginning to study the history of their family members who were descended from the original Native American Texans. Native American Texans were among the first settlers in the state. They are proud of the role they have played in the history of Texas and of the United States.